For Lexi Arrietta Bell and all kids
who love the Bay.

especially who
those who
visit the beach house
at
Goose Point
9/2005

Ever with love,
Jane
Anders

AWESOME CHESAPEAKE

A Kid's Guide to the Bay

By David Owen Bell

Illustrated By Marcy Dunn Ramsey

Tidewater Publishers
Centreville, Maryland

The author thanks teachers Joanne Frisch, Julie Gause,
and Lisa Pellicani for reviewing and grading the manuscript,
and Peter Rice of Echo Hill Outdoor School in Worton,
Maryland, for permission to use material that originally
appeared in *My Beachcombers' Guide to the Chesapeake Bay*
and *The Chesapeake BayGull*. The author also gratefully
acknowledges the influence of Echo Hill's teaching method
and philosophy, and hopes that this book will encourage
young people (and old) to have fun as they learn.

Contents

The Birth of the Bay

The Chesapeake Bay is fairly young in the overall history of this planet. It has only been around for about three thousand years. Its origin goes back to the last ice age when glaciers covered much of North America, reaching as far south as Pennsylvania.

Twenty thousand years ago, sea level was more than 300 feet lower than it is now. Virginia Beach and Ocean City would have been inland, many miles from the coast. The Susquehanna River flowed from what is now New York State through Maryland and southeastern Virginia to the Atlantic Ocean. Animals found food and shelter in marshes and meadows along the river valley. The Chesapeake Bay didn't exist.

Then, the earth began to warm slowly and the glaciers started to melt, returning water to the earth's oceans. As sea level rose, land was covered by water. About ten thousand years ago, the waters of the Atlantic Ocean began to flood the lower Susquehanna valley and form the Chesapeake Bay.

At about the same time, Native Americans reached the area on their long migration across the continent. They were descendants of the people who first came to North America along the land bridge that joined Alaska and Asia during the last ice age. They were the first, or native, Americans.

As sea level continued to rise, more of the valley was flooded, and the Bay grew northward. Five thousand years ago, the Bay reached the Annapolis area. By three thousand years ago, it had grown to about its present size.

The most recent ice age wasn't the first. There have been four in the last million years. Each time, as the earth's climate got colder, water from the ocean froze into glaciers that reached out from the polar ice caps and caused the sea level to drop. Each time, as the climate slowly warmed, melted water returned to the seas and raised their level. The Chesapeake Bay we know is not the first Bay, only the latest.

Today, the Susquehanna River still flows to the Chesapeake Bay, one of hundreds of rivers and creeks that constantly feed it fresh water. These are called tributaries. Fresh water also falls on the Bay as rain and snow and drains into the Bay from the land.

The Bay also gets salt water from the Atlantic Ocean. Twice a day, tides caused by the gravity of the moon and the sun carry salty ocean water into and out of the Bay as far as its northern end and well up the rivers. This mixture of fresh and salt water is called brackish water.

Brackish bodies of water that are connected to an ocean are called estuaries. Bodies of water that are partly surrounded by land are called bays. The Chesapeake Bay is an estuary of the Atlantic Ocean and the largest estuary in North America. Even as you read this, the Chesapeake Bay is changing shape. Waves are wearing away its edges, making it wider and shallower. Rivers, wind, and rainfall are bringing more sediment (small particles of soil and sand) that settles in and fills the Bay. This wearing away of land by water or wind is called erosion.

As people burn gas, coal, oil, and wood for transportation, electricity, and heat, we put more carbon dioxide in the air. Carbon dioxide traps heat from the sun and holds it in the atmosphere. This can cause our climate to grow gradually warmer, a process known as global warming. As this happens, more polar ice melts, and the sea level rises very slowly. So, while erosion is filling the Bay with more soil, global warming may be filling it with more water.

— That's a lot of H_2O !

That's the chemical name for WATER !

Just the Facts

✓ The Chesapeake Bay is almost 200 miles long and up to 30 miles wide.

✓ The Bay is home to over 2,500 species of animals and plants.

✓ The Bay covers 2,500 square miles and holds 18 trillion (that's 18,000,000,000,000) gallons of water.

✓ The average depth of the Bay itself is about 28 feet. Its greatest depth is 174 feet.

✓ The Chesapeake Bay watershed covers 64,000 square miles and is home to over 14 million people.

✓ Every day, people put about 1.5 billion gallons of treated sewage and four billion gallons of industrial waste into the Chesapeake Bay.

✓ A gallon of water weighs eight pounds. Imagine the force of the Susquehanna River's average flow of 19 million gallons a minute.

✓ Ninety percent of the Bay's fresh water comes from five of its tributaries: the Susquehanna, Potomac, York, James, and Rappahannock rivers.

What are the saltiest parts of the Bay?

✓ The southern part of the Bay is saltiest because it is closer to the ocean.

✓ The bottom is saltier because salt water is heavier than fresh water.

✓ Eastern Shore waters are saltier because the spinning of the earth causes salt water entering the Bay to curve toward the Eastern Shore, and because western shore rivers flow more power-fully, which also pushes the salt water to the east.

When is the Bay least or most salty?

✓ The Bay is least salty in the spring when rain and melting snow add more fresh water.

✓ It is saltiest in the fall when less fresh water flows into it. Also, the summer sun causes some Bay water to evaporate, leaving the salt behind.

HEY !

Quit a "SALT" in me!

A WEB OF LIFE

If you look across almost any body of water, the water will appear blue. The blue is a reflection of sunlight. Many rivers are brown. The muddy brown color is caused by soil in the water.

If you have the chance to look straight down at the Chesapeake Bay from a boat, pier, or bridge, you'll see that the water is green. It is green for the same reason that parks and forests and lawns are green: plants. These plants, called algae, are so small they can't be seen without a microscope.

Unlike other plants that get nourishment from nutrients in the soil through their roots, algae drift and get nourishment from nutrients in the water.

Like plants on land, plants in the Bay need water, sunlight, and carbon dioxide. Algae get sunlight that penetrates the surface of the water and carbon dioxide from fish and other animals that live in the water.

Life in the Chesapeake depends on algae. Because the Bay has so much algae, it can support many other forms of life in large numbers. Algae give off oxygen into the water that fish and crabs breathe. Much of this oxygen escapes into the air where it can be breathed by humans and other land animals. Larger plants, including weeds and grasses, also provide food and oxygen, as well as shelter for life in the Bay.

The web of life in the Chesapeake Bay (also called a food web) starts with drifting microscopic plants such as algae that are eaten by small drifting animals. Another name for

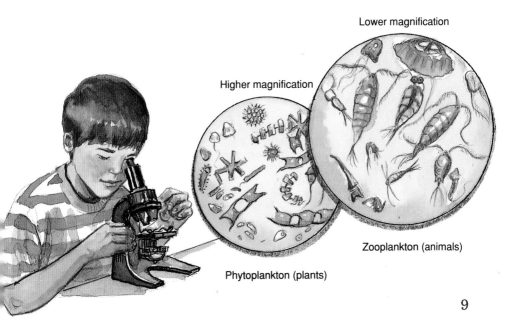

Lower magnification

Higher magnification

Zooplankton (animals)

Phytoplankton (plants)

drifters is plankton. Plant plankton and animal plankton are carried by the current. They go with the flow. Scientists call plant plankton "phytoplankton," and animal plankton "zooplankton."

Animal plankton include baby crabs and fish that are too small to swim against the current. Those that grow big and strong enough to swim where they want to are no longer plankton. Some kinds of animal plankton look like very tiny shrimp and will never grow any bigger.

Plant and animal plankton are eaten by clams, oysters, mussels, jellyfish, and small fish such as anchovies and silversides that strain or filter the water for food. These small fish are eaten by larger fish such as white perch, which are eaten by larger fish such as striped bass or bluefish.

A Simple Chesapeake Bay Food Web

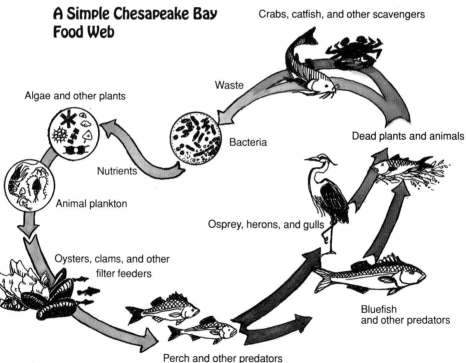

Crabs, catfish, and other scavengers

Algae and other plants

Waste

Bacteria

Dead plants and animals

Nutrients

Animal plankton

Osprey, herons, and gulls

Oysters, clams, and other filter feeders

Bluefish and other predators

Perch and other predators

Clams and mussels are eaten by crabs and catfish. Fish are eaten by great blue herons, eagles, ospreys, and gulls. People eat fish, clams, crabs, and oysters. When Bay animals eat, they make waste, just like people do. The waste ends up on the bottom along with the remains of dead plants and animals, called detritus (de-TRY-tus). Bacteria decompose the waste and detritus, breaking them down into simple nutrients that are used by plants, and the Chesapeake Bay food web is complete with producers (plants), consumers (animals), and decomposers (bacteria).

The Chesapeake Bay and the rivers that feed it are surrounded by land. Soil gets into the water and provides nutrients that help the algae grow. Some rivers look brown because they have too much soil in them. Some water looks clear because it doesn't have enough soil in it for algae to grow.

Clear water is often found near sandy beaches on islands and ocean coastlines. Sand doesn't have the nutrients that soil does, so sandy water isn't as good a place for plants to grow. Without algae, there aren't as many animal plankton. Without animal plankton, there aren't as many fish.

Clear water looks good, but it doesn't support as much life as green water does. Clear water can be thought of as a desert and green water as a jungle teeming with life. Healthy estuaries are full of life.

Most of the life in the ocean depends on estuaries as a place to be born, to grow up, to feed, or as a source for food. The Chesapeake Bay is a root of the Atlantic Ocean, giving it food and supporting its life.

People and the Chesapeake Bay

Over 14 million people live in the Chesapeake watershed. A watershed is the area of land that drains into a body of water. The Chesapeake watershed includes the District of Columbia, most of Maryland, much of Pennsylvania and Virginia, and parts of Delaware, West Virginia, and New York State.

This area's rainfall and melted snow flow into the Bay or the streams and rivers that feed it. The air above the Chesapeake Bay is also important. Pollution in the airshed ends up in the Bay when rainfall brings it back to earth.

Rainwater that is not absorbed by the land runs off it. Falling rain and runoff take other things along with them, such as fertilizers and pesticides from farms and gardens, leaked motor oil from roads and driveways, household chemicals, and factory waste.

Fertilizers contain natural or chemical nutrients to help plants and crops grow. When people put fertilizer on lawns and fields, rain washes it into rivers and streams that feed the Bay. Factory, power plant, and automobile exhausts contain chemical nutrients that come back to earth when it rains. These also find their way to the Bay.

Sewage plants and septic systems clean waste water from homes, schools, and businesses. The treated water that is discharged into waterways or seeps into ground water also contains nutrients.

Plenty of erosion occurs naturally all around the Chesapeake Bay, but people make it worse by cutting down trees,

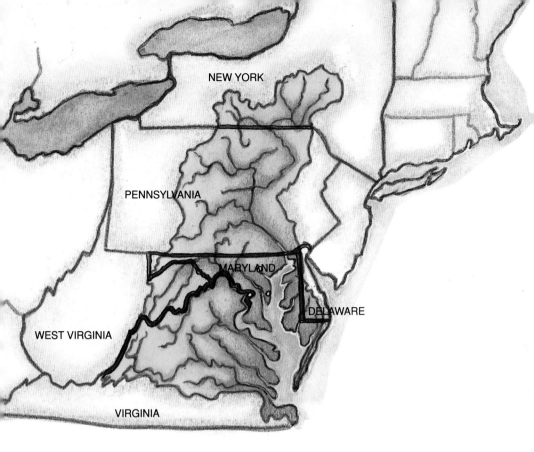

NEW YORK

PENNSYLVANIA

MARYLAND

DELAWARE

WEST VIRGINIA

VIRGINIA

plowing fields, paving highways, and filling in wetlands. When people destroy woodlands and wetlands to build homes, roads, and shopping centers, they limit nature's ability to absorb and filter water as it runs off the land.

Too much soil in the water can smother fish eggs and small animals or clog the gills through which they get their oxygen. It also keeps sunlight from reaching underwater plants that provide animals with food and shelter, so these plants die.

Since the Chesapeake Bay and its tributaries are surrounded by land, enough nutrients from eroded soil, dead plants and animals, and animal waste naturally end up in the estuary. This gives the algae plenty of nutrients and the Bay plenty of algae to support the web of life.

Today, the Chesapeake Bay is threatened because it gets too many nutrients. Too many nutrients from erosion, run-off, exhaust, and sewage (over 400,000 pounds a day) can cause too much algae to grow, blocking sunlight that underwater plants need. When there's more algae than the animal plankton and filter feeders can eat, much of it dies and ends up on the bottom to decompose. The bacteria use up more and more of the limited supply of oxygen in the water as they decompose the dead algae, and animals start dying.

Sudden growths of too much algae, called blooms or green tides, often happen in the springtime when heavy rains carry large amounts of newly applied fertilizers and freshly plowed soil to streams, rivers, ponds, and estuaries. Pesticides and other toxic chemicals that are harmful to life also enter the water just when newly hatched fish, birds, and other animals are weakest.

YUK!

Acid Rain

Rain water is naturally slightly acidic because of the carbon dioxide it picks up as it forms and falls to earth. The weak acid rain dissolves minerals in the earth (salt, calcium, iron, and zinc, for example) and carries them to creeks, rivers, and eventually the oceans. Some of these minerals neutralize the rain water's acidity.

Burning fossil fuels, such as coal, oil, and gasoline, to heat homes, generate electricity, and run cars, puts sulphur and nitrogen oxides into the air where they form sulfuric and nitric acids which mix with rain. This stronger acid rain is harmful to plant and animal life.

Everyone Can Help

Here's how to be a good citizen of the Chesapeake Bay watershed:

✓ Plant trees and shrubs around your home or school to help hold the soil and slow runoff.

✓ Save electricity. Use it only when you need it. Power plants that burn coal or oil add chemical nutrients to the airshed.

✓ Share rides, take the bus, or ride your bike. Car exhaust also puts chemical nutrients into the air and contributes to acid rain.

✓ Recycle and buy things made from recycled materials. Recycling saves natural resources and energy and helps reduce pollution from factory and power plant exhausts.

✓ Avoid mowing, watering, and fertilizing your lawn too much.

✓ Tell people what you think. Many parents, friends, teachers, and even elected officials will listen to you. (For example, the next item on this list was suggested by a four-year-old.)

✓ Don't litter. Litter looks bad and can also be harmful to animal life.

✓ Be responsible for your waste. Make sure that household chemicals, motor oil, and paint get disposed of properly so they don't end up in a river or bay.

✓ Conserve water to help keep wastewater treatment systems working right.

✓ Enjoy visiting and learning about the Chesapeake Bay and its tributaries.

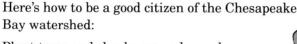

Life Around the Chesapeake Bay

Bivalve

Gastropod

Life in and around the Chesapeake Bay falls into two broad categories: plants and animals. Animals are classified either as vertebrates (with a spine, or backbone) or as invertebrates (without a spine).

Vertebrates include mammals, birds, reptiles, amphibians, and fish. Invertebrates include jellyfish, hydroids, sponges, worms, mollusks, and arthropods. The two major classes of mollusks in the Bay are gastropods (single-shelled animals such as snails and whelks) and bivalves (clams, oysters, mussels, and other mollusks with two shells).

Arthropods are animals with jointed legs and a shell that serves as its outer support, or exoskeleton. They grow by shedding their shells and growing new, larger ones. Arthropods fall into two main types: one including spiders, scorpions, and horseshoe crabs, and the other including insects and crustaceans. Shrimp, amphipods, barnacles, and most crabs fall into the crustacean class.

Aquatic animal life is also described as being either plankton (drifters), nekton (swimmers), or benthos (bottom dwellers). Plankton ranges from small shrimplike copepods to jellyfish and also includes the larvae of larger animals that will become nekton or benthos once they mature.

The nekton is made up mostly of all the fish that travel the Bay. The benthic community includes clams, oysters, and the many worms, burrowing crustaceans, and bacteria that live in the bottom mud.

The plants and animals included in this guide were chosen because they are interesting or they are important to the ecology of the Bay. Most of them can be found all around the Bay, but life varies from the fresh water of the upper Bay and rivers to the salty ocean water at its mouth, and the mixed or brackish water in between. This makes the Chesapeake a great place to explore, learn, and have fun.

Life Along the Shore

Whether a sand beach, mud flat, or marsh, the shoreline is a special place where land and water meet, and where we can find living animals and signs of life not seen anywhere else, as well as things brought from far away by winds or currents.

Although sandy beaches don't support as much life as other places (they lack plants that provide food material and shelter), a public beach may be the easiest way for you to get to the Bay. Beaches are most often thought of as places to swim and play, but with a little time and patience, you can discover a whole community living there.

Moving water forms beaches by depositing sand and minerals on the shore, and it makes mud flats by leaving behind fine particles of dirt. Water can change the shape and size of beaches and flats slowly over time or quickly in a severe storm.

High and low tides come to the Chesapeake twice a day. Tides are caused by the gravitational pull of the moon and sun. The tide first covers and then exposes part of the land. Between the low and high tide lines is the intertidal zone: the best place to look for life along the shore. The best time to explore the shoreline is when the tide is out, especially after a storm or when the moon is new or full and the tide is lower than usual.

Once the home of a live animal, a shell is usually the first thing to catch the beachcomber's eye. Gastropod shells are cone-shaped. If you hold the shell facing you with the spire, or twisted end, up and the opening is on your right, then you have a right-handed shell, the more common kind. Left-handed shells are much harder to find.

Other possible finds are single or paired bivalve shells still held together by their ligament. Round scars on the insides of the shells show where the muscles that used to open and close them were once attached.

Many people also enjoy looking for stones, driftwood, bird feathers, or some rare and unusual find such as a fossilized shark tooth. The only tools you really need are your eyes and hands, but a shovel and sifter can help. Look carefully in shaded or covered places and tide pools, and respect living things and their homes.

Right   Left

AMPHIPOD

These small crustaceans are found just about everywhere and include the beach hoppers and fleas that live in and around the sand and the scuds that live in the mud at the bottom of the Bay. At the beach, look for them sleeping in the sand or under the row of dry weeds at the high tide line during the day or feeding near the water's edge at night. Other amphipods can be found by sifting through a shovelful of mud or shaking a crab trap, old bottle, or anything that has been in the water long enough to get something growing on it.

Some amphipods filter the water for plankton; others help decompose dead plants and animals. They provide food for fish and birds.

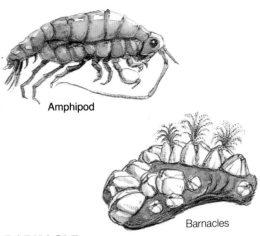
Amphipod

FIDDLER CRAB

The male fiddler crab uses its large claw to wave off enemies and attract mates with a back-and-forth motion. Most species live in mud flats, feeding on dead plant matter when the tide is out and returning to their burrows when it is in. They can get their oxygen from the air as long as their gills are wet. At night, fiddlers seal the entrances to their burrows with mud.

Barnacles

BARNACLE

All around the Bay in the late spring, barnacle larvae by the billions pour out of their parents' shells. Many of these young drifters are eaten by filter feeders. Those that survive live on plankton and grow by molting, or shedding, their shells for bigger ones.

Then, with one of nature's strongest glues, the barnacle attaches itself to a boat or ship bottom, rock, piling, shell, piece of driftwood, bottle, can, and at sea, even a whale. Once attached, it sticks for life.

A barnacle that is exposed at low tide will close its valve to keep from drying out. If you find a barnacle on a small object, try putting it in a glass of brackish water and watch it open and reach for plankton and small particles of food with its feet.

Barnacle wise guy...

TAG! You're IT!

21

GREAT BLUE HERON

Once hunted for its feathers, the great blue heron is now a common sight along the shores of the Chesapeake Bay and tributaries. Wading in shallow water, it thrusts with its bill to catch fish, crustaceans, worms, and insects.

CANVASBACK DUCK

Along with other waterfowl, the canvasback winters on the Chesapeake and other mid-Atlantic estuaries. Its strong legs set well back on its body make it a powerful diver in the water but awkward on land.

The canvasback favors aquatic grasses (wild celery and sago pondweed) in its diet, but with the decline of these plants and the habitat that supports them, now eats small clams. This change in diet has changed the way the duck tastes and has made it less attractive as a meal for humans who once hunted it in great numbers.

TERRAPIN

The northern diamondback terrapin is a turtle that favors brackish marshes. Protective scales help keep its skin moist. It eats mollusks, crustaceans, insects, and fish. Terrapin were once hunted nearly to extinction for their tasty meat. Left alone, they can live forty years or more.

Turtles are hatched from eggs. Their shell grows as they do. The diamondback has webbed feet for swimming and strong, sharp jaws that make up for its lack of teeth.

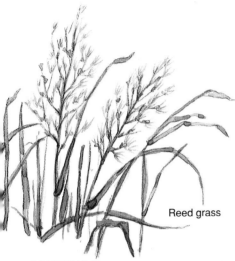
Reed grass

REED GRASS

Also known as phragmites (frag-MY-deez), reed grass often crowds out other shoreline plants that would provide nourishment to animals that live there. Once established, its underground stems grow outward quickly.

SALTMARSH CORDGRASS

Also called spartina, this plant gives life to the marsh, a habitat or living place that most fish depend on during part of their lives to mate, feed, or find shelter. Spartina helps keep the bottom in place and provides a habitat for birds and animals to feed and nest. As dead bits of the plant fall to the bottom of the marsh, they provide a major source of detritus which fuels the food web.

Marshland is a valuable resource that produces more tons of protein per acre than farmland. People have destroyed many acres of marshland for development and to get rid of pests (mosquitoes and flies).

Saltmarsh cordgrass

MUSKRAT

A common aquatic rodent found in fresh and brackish ponds, creeks, and marshes, the muskrat eats plant stems, clams, and insects. It builds dome-shaped homes of mud and grass which it enters and exits under water.

A muskrat can sometimes be seen swimming on the surface. Foxes and other upland predators come to the marsh to hunt it. Except for its hairless tail, the muskrat is covered by thick oily fur.

OSPREY

Also called a fish hawk, the osprey spends about half of the year around the Chesapeake Bay, arriving here in the spring from South America, where it winters.

Returning pairs of males and females usually find their old nest sites on trees or the red and green channel markers that guide boats through the rivers and harbors around the Bay. They repair their nests or build new ones of sticks. There they will incubate their eggs and care for their hatchlings until they are old enough to fly.

Osprey hover over the water looking for fish. They descend on their prey and grab it with their talons.

GULL

The herring gull lives all around the estuary and is what people commonly call a "seagull." It has a great appetite and will eat anything it can get, from garbage to shellfish. The growing number of herring gulls is bad news for other marine birds because herring gulls take over their nesting areas and eat their eggs.

Herring gulls can be found anywhere from garbage dumpsters to the open water. They sometimes drop crabs or mussels on rocks to break the shells so they can feast on the animal inside.

BALD EAGLE

Once threatened by the widespread use of the pesticide DDT, the bald eagle is making a comeback around the Chesapeake Bay. DDT caused the birds to lay eggs with shells so thin that they broke before the young could hatch. Since the pesticide was banned, the bald eagle population has been on the rise.

Pairs of eagles nest in high treetops along the shore. They eat mostly fish, but also snakes, turtles, and small animals. Young bald eagles are dark brown with specks of white. At four to five years they mature and get the white head that gives them their name.

Not SEA gull, BAYgull!

bagel?

24

Life in the Water

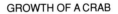

People swimming or wading in shallow water usually don't give much thought to the life around them until they feel a light and quick nibble on the toe or the sting of a sea nettle on the leg. Shallow water can be full of living things that are hard to see because they are small, quick, transparent, or camouflaged. Shrimp, clams, snails, and schools of tiny fish are common. Dragging a seine net or minnow net along the shore can bring up a rich haul. A net can be easily made with about five feet of window screen stretched between two poles.

Even though deeper water is home to life people don't normally see unless they go fishing, signs of this life often make it to shore. Mollusk shells, cast-off crab shells, and the remains of large fish often get washed up on beaches.

BLUE CRAB

The crab is big business around the Chesapeake Bay. Millions and millions of pounds are caught every year by commercial and recreational crabbers.

A fearless omnivore, the blue crab will eat whatever it can catch, including newly dead fish, snails, clams, plants, and its own soft-shelled cousins. As a crab grows, it sheds its shell, or molts. Until its new shell hardens, it is defenseless. Cast-off shells are often washed up along the shore.

Crabs mate in summer and early fall. Males spend the winter in the deep mud. Females migrate

GROWTH OF A CRAB

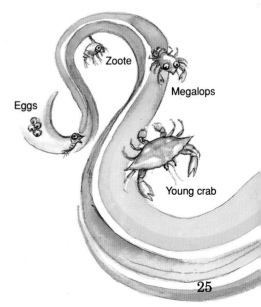

Eggs

Zoote

Megalops

Young crab

to the salty mouth of the Bay where in the spring they release their "sponges" of up to two million eggs. After the eggs hatch, the crabs grow quickly, molting as often as every few days at first until they reach maturity in as little as one year. Out of the two million eggs, only a few will reach adulthood. Most are eaten by other animals.

Live crabs are green and blue on top and white on the bottom. Looked at from above, they blend with the water. Viewed from below, they blend with the sunlight. Females and young males have red-tipped claws ("painted fingernails") as a signal to mature males not to attack. When crabs are steamed for eating, or cast-off shells are baked by the sun, a chemical reaction causes the shell to turn red.

On the bottom of the crab, the male's apron is long and thin, like the Washington Monument. The female's is built for holding eggs and is shorter and rounded, like the Capitol Dome. An immature female's apron is triangular.

Admired for its feisty disposition, enjoyable eating, and abundance, the blue crab is one of the most popular symbols of the Chesapeake Bay. Its Latin name, *Callinectes sapidus,* means beautiful swimmer.

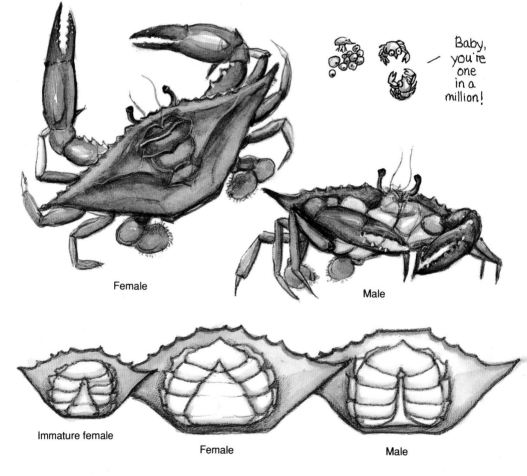

Baby, you're one in a million!

Female

Male

Immature female

Female

Male

FISH-GILL ISOPOD

Look for this parasite under the gill covers of white perch and other fish. The fish-gill isopod grasps onto the gills of the fish, growing faster than it does.

Fish-gill isopod

COMB JELLY

These small transparent plankton-eating blobs, members of the jelly-fish family, do not sting. Also called sea walnuts, they are easier to see in a glass of water, or at night when, once disturbed, they give off a phosphorescent green glow, similar to a firefly.

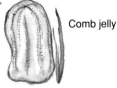

Comb jelly

SPONGE

A sponge is a colony of simple tiny animals held together and supported by spongy fiber. Like sea squirts and other filter feeders, sponges pump water in and out, filtering it for plankton and other microscopic bits of food.

Chesapeake sponges grow on underwater rocks and pilings. The redbeard sponge is one of the Bay's most widespread species.

Sponge

Sea nettle

SEA NETTLE

This jellyfish is among the oldest forms of life on earth. Poison in the stinging cells of its tentacles stuns small fish and stings swimmers that blunder into its way. Carried by the current, it is capable of some movement by pulsating its mushroomlike top, which can be safely held by hand since it does not have stinging cells.

The sea nettle will eat whatever it can get, but relies heavily on animal plankton in its diet. It is all too common throughout the summer and early fall in all but the freshest waters.

SEA SQUIRT

Sea squirts

Looking like bunches of dull green grapes, sea squirts attach to rocks, shells, and underwater pilings. They pump water in one spout and out the other, getting food and oxygen and expelling waste in the process.

So many plankton,
So little time....

HERMIT CRAB

This crustacean resembles a lobster, but its soft belly, exposed and unprotected, is a tempting target for predators. The hermit crab finds shelter by borrowing an empty shell or eating its way into one already occupied.

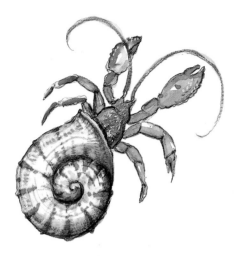

As the crab grows, it must find bigger and bigger shells in which to dwell. It uses two pairs of legs to keep itself in its shell, two pairs of legs for walking, and one clawed pair for feeding and defense.

The hermit crab is an omnivorous scavenger—eating just about anything it comes across. It is found in the saltier southern third of the Bay.

SHRIMP

Although there aren't enough large ones for humans to bother with, shrimp can be found throughout the Chesapeake Bay. Like crabs, they belong to the crustacean order Decapoda (ten legs). Of the different species of shrimp in the Bay, some are predators, some eat plankton, and some eat detritus. Shrimp provide food for fish.

Small sand shrimp and common grass shrimp can be caught by pulling a fine net through the water along the beach and around underwater plants.

Is this shell for rent yet?

NO!

28

HORSESHOE CRAB

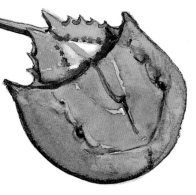

Although more closely related to a spider than a crab, the horseshoe crab has five pairs of legs. The first four have claws at the tips and grinding joints where they join the body at the mouth. The grinders only work while the legs are moving, so the crab must walk to eat its diet of small mollusks, worms, and detritus. Its fifth pair of clawless legs is used to propel it along the bottom. Its long tail is used for balance and steering, and for turning itself right side up when it gets flipped over.

Once ground up for fertilizer and animal feed, the horseshoe crab has found a new career in medicine. Its shell is used to make the special dressings that protect victims of severe burns from infection. Its blue blood (copper-based rather than iron-based like red blood) has an element that may stop the growth of some cancer cells and can detect the presence of certain poisons and disease.

The horseshoe crab had already been around for millions of years when dinosaurs roamed the earth. It molts by leaving its shell through a slit in the front. Cast-off shells can be found along the shore.

HYDROID

Attached to firm underwater surfaces, their branches growing out to stems with flowery tips, hydroids look like plants, but they are actually colonies of animals. The individual animals, called zooids, live in stemlike tubes. Tiny flowery tops stick out at the ends. These hydranths have tentacles with stinging cells that paralyze their prey and feed it to a mouth in the center of the "flower." The food is moved into the stems and throughout the colony.

Hydroids can be found on rocks, pilings, and shells underwater. Taken out of water, the tentacles retract into the tube. Put back into water, they re-emerge.

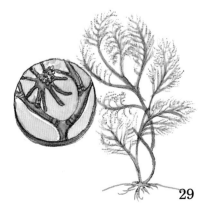

Maybe he should just yell "FIRE!" under water?

29

CLAM

Razor, jackknife, soft-shelled, macoma, and surf clams are among the many kinds of clams that live throughout the Bay. The hard clam, or quahog (KWAW-hawg), shell was used by Native Americans for jewelry and money.

Most clams have two siphons that stick up out of their shells. Water is sucked in one and pumped out the other. The clam extracts plankton and oxygen and expels carbon dioxide and waste. Clams move up and down in the mud with the help of a single tongue-shaped foot.

Clams are eaten by fish, birds, and crabs. Many are harvested and shipped to New England, where they are enjoyed fried and in chowders.

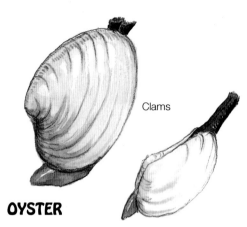

Clams

MUSSEL

Mussels

The mussel is a filter feeding bivalve. Of the several species found around the Chesapeake, the hooked mussel has the greatest range. It attaches to hard surfaces with threads that it secretes. The mussel can then pull and slacken these threads to gain a small bit of movement.

OYSTER

As oyster larvae grow, they settle and attach to a firm surface—usually another, older oyster. Once attached, they don't move. Generations of oysters live on top of and next to each other on firm bottoms in brackish water. Healthy oyster bars are thriving communities alive with worms, snails, squirts, small fish and crabs, mussels, and barnacles. Oysters filter the water for plant plankton. Most oysters spend their first year as males and by age two become females.

Oysters have long been an important fishery on the Chesapeake Bay. Today, oysters are threatened by diseases that kill them before they reach market size of three inches. The yearly catch is a small fraction of what it once was.

Oyster bar

WORM

Worms are digging and boring all through the bottom of the Bay, churning up the mud as they eat their way through, digesting whatever organic material they can. Their waste makes for a richer, more nutritious bottom mud.

Some worms live in tubes that they build, others wander over the mud flats. Worms are an important source of food for birds, fish, and crabs.

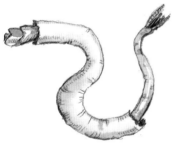

SHIPWORM

This mollusk (not really a worm) uses the edges of its shells to dig through submerged wood. Wooden boats, pilings, and driftwood are all fair game for the shipworm.

The shipworm prefers the saltier water of the mid- to lower Bay, but driftwood found on beaches throughout the Bay can be broken open to reveal the shipworm's tunnels.

SNAIL

Whelks, periwinkles, and snails are single-shelled animals classed as gastropods (stomach foot). They have a large tongue-shaped "foot" that moves them along the bottom. Glands on their underside secrete a mucus to help them glide.

Most Chesapeake Bay snails have gills for getting oxygen out of the water. If caught out of water by an ebbing tide, they pull back their bodies and close the entrance to their shell so they won't dry out.

Some snails feed on algae and detritus, others are carnivores (animal-eaters). The moon snail drills holes in clamshells to eat the animal inside.

Slugs and nudibranchs are snails without shells. In the Chesapeake they are small (less than one inch) and are found mostly feeding on and around underwater plants in the saltier half of the Bay.

Worm dating...

Haven't I seen you somewhere before?

Finish your algae, children, or you won't get any detritus!

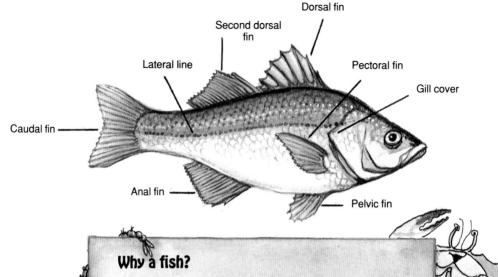

Dorsal fin

Second dorsal fin

Lateral line

Pectoral fin

Gill cover

Caudal fin

Anal fin

Pelvic fin

Why a fish?

✓ A fish is a cold-blooded vertebrate with fins. Most fish are covered with scales to protect their skin. The scales are covered by a coat of slime that protects the fish from bacteria. Fish absorb oxygen from the water through their gills.

✓ Fish have a lateral line running from head to tail along each side of the body. With it, they sense vibrations and waves that are built up as they pass solid objects or that are sent out by other moving things. Lateral lines enable fish to sense unseen predators and food, and to turn instantly with other fish in schools.

✓ A fish's fins are for stability and motion. The dorsal and anal fins keep the fish upright. The caudal, pelvic, and pectoral fins are for moving, turning, and stopping.

✓ Most fish in the Chesapeake Bay are greenish on top and white on the bottom. This natural camouflage helps them elude predators.

✓ Fish are the world's oldest vertebrates, evolving from mud-sucking wrigglers over the last 400 million years. The Chesapeake Bay and its tributaries are home to some 200 species.

why are fish so smart?

What do you call a fish scientist?

An Icthiologist

Because they travel in schools !

Catfish comedian

EEL

Born in the Sargasso Sea, a region of the Atlantic Ocean, eel larvae make their way to North America and to the rivers, creeks, and estuaries where they will grow. Several years later, mature eels head back to the same area of the ocean to breed. They won't eat during their long journey and will die when it's over, but will have given birth to a new generation.

The eel is a long fish with scales and fins. It is a nocturnal feeder, hunting just about anything from amphipods to fish, crabs, and clams while spending its days resting in the mud.

CATFISH

Catfish use their whiskers to feel for food along the dark and muddy bottom of the rivers and upper Chesapeake Bay. They move upstream to fresh water to spawn. The males protect their offspring until they grow large enough to make it on their own.

Smooth and slimy, catfish lack scales but have sharp spines in their fins and should be handled with care.

HOG CHOKER

This small flatfish starts life swimming upright with an eye on each side of its head. As the hog choker develops, its left eye migrates to the right side of its head until it is next to the right eye. Meanwhile, the fish starts to swim on its side. Its left side becomes its bottom and its right side becomes its top.

Hog chokers lie partly buried in the mud, their brown mottled top providing the camouflage they need as their beady eyes look up for food. Although they are found throughout the estuary, the story goes that because they didn't have other uses, these plentiful fish were once fed to hogs.

Catfish

Hog Choker

Eel

BLUEFISH

A ravenous predator with strong jaws and sharp teeth, the bluefish comes to the Bay from the Atlantic Ocean in the spring to dine on anchovies and menhaden. It moves back to the salty ocean by the end of autumn.

Bluefish

Cownose ray

COWNOSE RAY

Along with sharks and skates, rays have skeletons made of cartilage instead of bone, like other vertebrates.

Cownose rays use their powerful fins to stir up the bottom hunting soft-shelled clams and destroying underwater plants in the process. With their large size (up to three feet), powerful mouth, and poisonous spine near their tail, rays have little to fear.

ANCHOVY

These small sleek fish forage for tiny bits of food. Traveling in schools, the fishes' silver streaks sometimes catch the eye as they turn away.

Anchovies are found from shallows close to shore to deep open water where they are hunted by bluefish and striped bass. Another small silver-striped fish, the silverside, is also abundant in shallow waters around the Bay.

Anchovies

MENHADEN

Too oily for humans to eat, this fish still has commercial value as animal feed and fertilizer. Its oil is used in paints and other products.

Born in the ocean, schools of menhaden come to the Chesapeake to filter the water for plankton. They are hunted by bluefish and other predators.

Menhaden

KILLIFISH

Killifish, minnows, and mummichogs are among the species of small fish that live in shallow shoreline waters from spring through fall. In the winter, they move to deeper water which holds heat longer. Traveling in schools helps them find food and avoid larger predators.

Mummichogs eat living and dead plants and animals, including amphipods, shrimp, and mosquito larvae. Striped killifish can be found along sandy beaches, sometimes trying to flop back into the water after being caught by an outgoing tide.

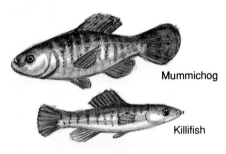

Mummichog

Killifish

SEAHORSE

Seahorses are found in grass meadows in the southern half of the Bay. The female places her eggs in the male's pouch and they are hatched from there. Seahorses swim upright and wrap their tails around plant leaves to feed on small organisms.

Seahorse

SHAD

Shad and other herrings are born in the fresh upper reaches of the Bay's tidal tributaries. The young slowly move downstream as they grow, migrating to the ocean by fall. They roam the Atlantic in schools until they mature at about four years. Then they return to the stream where they were born to spawn a new generation.

From colonial times through the first part of this century, tons of shad were harvested during their annual spawning runs. They are not so common now. Modern dams and roads that block the rivers have kept them from reaching their spawning grounds. Now, fish lifts alongside the dams on the Susquehanna River may enable more shad to complete their journey.

STRIPED BASS

Also known locally as rockfish, stripers spawn in the fresh and brackish tidal waters of Chesapeake Bay rivers and creeks. Young males mostly live and feed in their home waters, but many of the females and older males migrate to the ocean to mature. They range from Canada to Florida and return to the Bay as adults to spawn.

Striped bass larvae are sensitive to toxins, as are the animal plankton that the young fish eat. Chlorine that is used to treat sewage and other waste water is especially harmful. Striped bass were once a major fishery on the Chesapeake Bay, but a sharp decline in their population forced a fishing ban that is gradually being lifted as the fish shows signs of a comeback.

The Chesapeake is the spawning ground and nursery for an estimated ninety percent of the Atlantic striped bass population. A striped bass caught off the coast of Maine was probably born on a tributary of the Bay.

SEAWEED

Like plants on land, weeds growing in the water provide oxygen, food, and habitat for animals. Life depends on them.

In some parts of the world, seaweed is harvested from coastal waters for use as food and as a blending agent called algin which is found in candy bars, soup, toothpaste, and ice cream.

Weeds in the estuary are larger cousins of the microscopic planktonic algae. They aren't rooted, but attach to the bottom and other firm surfaces with holdfasts. Like algae, they get nourishment from nutrients in the water and need sunlight to grow.

Storms pull Bay weeds and other plants from their holdfasts and wash them ashore. Look for them in a row along the high tide line.

WHITE PERCH

Adult white perch migrate upstream for the spring spawning, then downstream for the summer to feed, then to the deep relatively warmer water for the winter. Perch are found throughout the Chesapeake Bay, but as loyal residents of the estuary, never on the ocean.

Fun-dex

Name the plant or animal identified in each clue. If you need a hint, match the letter of the clue with the page number to its right in the answer key. For more of a challenge, match the clue with the number of the plant or animal in the illustration, then compare your answer to the number and name in the answer key on page 40.

a. Lies on its back, eats with its feet.

b. Always looking for a new home.

c. Prehistoric creature eats on the run.

d. Native American currency.

e. It could be a pizza topping.

f. Their schools are always in session.

g. Four feet tall, six feet wide, weighs only six pounds.

h. Smooths its way with a path of ooze.

i. Makes its own thread.

j. National symbol favors the Chesapeake.

k. Senior citizen of the estuary.

l. The darker it gets, the easier they are to see.

m. Springtime invader.

n. Adults return to their birthplace—if we let them.

o. Can be found in candy bars, soup, toothpaste, and ice cream.

p. Strong flier, deep diver, clumsy walker.

q. Don't try taking a bath with this one.

r. Lives in a wooden condo.

s. Father watches whiskered babies.

t. From sandy beach to murky depths.

u. Its home is often painted red or green.

v. Its life begins and ends at sea.

w. No taste for salt.

x. Their lives are boring.

y. Mostly water, it's the estuary's largest plankton.

z. They wave some away and some close.

aa. Tasty beautiful swimmer.

bb. It really sees eye to eye.

cc. Life-giving plant.

dd. More likely to end up in a paint can than on a dinner table.

ee. Nature's water gun.

ff. Link between land and water.

gg. Uses its fins to find food.

hh. Noisy scavenger.

ii. Females travel, males stay home.

jj. Filters up to ten gallons of water an hour.

kk. Lives up to its name.

ll. When one eats, they all eat.

mm. Grows all around the Bay but not in it.

nn. Hangs on to its host.

oo. Father hatches eggs.

Answer Key

Clue	Page Number	Illustration Number	Name
a	21	22	barnacle
b	28	13	hermit crab
c	29	35	horseshoe crab
d	30	4	clam
e	34	27	anchovy
f	35	41	killifish
g	22	1	great blue heron
h	31	8	snail
i	30	31	mussel
j	24	18	bald eagle
k	22	38	terrapin
l	27	6	comb jelly
m	34	10	bluefish
n	36	24	shad
o	37	16	seaweed
p	22	29	canvasback duck
q	27	36	sponge
r	31	3	shipworm
s	33	14	catfish
t	21	33	amphipod
u	24	17	osprey
v	33	20	eel
w	37	30	white perch
x	31	7	worm
y	27	26	sea nettle
z	21	37	fiddler crab
aa	25	40	blue crab
bb	33	11	hog choker
cc	23	2	saltmarsh cordgrass
dd	35	5	menhaden
ee	27	21	sea squirt
ff	23	9	muskrat
gg	34	28	cownose ray
hh	24	23	gull
ii	36	12	striped bass
jj	30	34	oyster
kk	28	19	shrimp
ll	29	15	hydroid
mm	23	39	reed grass
nn	27	32	fish-gill isopod
oo	35	25	seahorse

Learning More

For Younger Readers

Blackistone, Mick. *The Day They Left the Bay*. Annapolis, Md.: Blue Crab Press, 1991.

Cummings, Priscilla. The *Chadwick* series. Centreville, Md.: Tidewater Publishers.

For Older Readers

Horton, Tom. *Bay Country*. Baltimore: The Johns Hopkins University Press, 1987.

Lippson, A.J. and R. L. Lippson. *Life in the Chesapeake*. Baltimore: The Johns Hopkins University Press, 1984.

Peterson Field Guide Series, various titles. Boston: Houghton Mifflin Company.

Warner, William. *Beautiful Swimmers*. Boston: Little, Brown & Company, 1976.

White, Christopher. *Chesapeake Bay: Nature of the Estuary, A Field Guide*. Centreville, Md.: Tidewater Publishers, 1989.

Williams, John Page, Jr. *Chesapeake Almanac: Following the Bay through the Seasons*. Centreville, Md.: Tidewater Publishers, 1993.

Video

"It's Happening Today on the Chesapeake Bay" with Billy B., Echo Hill Outdoor School, Worton, Maryland.

Index